no matter what

30 DEVOTIONS ON DECLARING JOY
IN ALL CIRCUMSTANCES

LIFEWAY GIRLS | DEVOTIONS

ISBN 978-1-0877-4088-1
Item 005831339
Dewey Decimal Classification Number: 242
Subject Heading: DEVOTIONAL LITERATURE / BIBLE STUDY AND
TEACHING / GOD

publishing team

Director, Student Ministry
Ben Trueblood

Manager, Student Ministry
Publishing
John Paul Basham

Editorial Team Leader
Karen Daniel

Editor
Stephanie Cross

Graphic Designer
Kaitlin Redmond

Printed in the United States of America

Student Ministry Publishing
LifeWay Resources
One LifeWay Plaza
Nashville, Tennessee 37234

We believe that the Bible has God for its author; salvation for its
end; and truth, without any mixture of error, for its matter and that
all Scripture is totally true and trustworthy. To review LifeWay's doc-
trinal guideline, please visit www.lifeway.com/doctrinalguideline.

Unless otherwise noted, all Scripture quotations are taken from the
Christian Standard Bible®, Copyright © 2017 by Holman Bible Publishers. Used by permission. Christian Standard Bible® and CSB®
are federally registered trademarks of Holman Bible Publishers.

04
Intro

05
Getting Started

06
Where does joy
come from?

18
What does real joy look like?

30
Why do people
get depressed?

40
How should Christians respond
to depression?

50
How can real joy
overcome depression?

64
What do you do when
being joyful is hard?

table of contents

If you went to a dance, to see a movie, or shopping with your friends, you'd probably really enjoy it. The next day you might remember the fun you had and smile, but it wouldn't be the same as being there. A few weeks later the smile that experience brought you might fade. Eventually, you might completely forget about it. What was fun for a moment, didn't bring you real, lasting joy.

Joy can be difficult to understand, and honestly, many people struggle with it. Some believe joy means fun, but they're not the same. Joy doesn't fade or diminish over time. We can experience joy in good times and bad. Joy is not rooted in our circumstances. Joy isn't determined by other people, what they think about us, or our relationship to them. Real and lasting joy—what the Bible sometimes calls delight—comes from somewhere else entirely.

We all want to understand joy. We want to know where to find it, how to experience it, and how to help others be joyful too.

Over the next 30 days, we will take a look at what the Bible says about joy, depression, and key truths about cultivating joy that fulfills and endures.

God's Word speaks clearly about joy, so let's take a look at what He says.

getting started

This devotional contains 30 days of content, divided into sections that each answer a specific question related to joy. Each day is broken down into three elements—discover, delight, and display—to help you answer core questions related to Scripture.

discover | This section helps you examine the passage in light of who God is and determine what it says about your identity in relationship to Him. Included here is the key passage and focus Scripture, along with illustrations and commentary to guide you as you study.

delight | In this section, you'll be challenged by questions and activities that help you see how God is alive and active in every detail of His Word and your life. You'll be guided to ask yourself what the passage means when it comes to your relationship with God.

display | Here's where you really take action. Display calls you to apply what you've learned from each day's study.

prayer | Each day also includes a prayer activity in one of the three main sections.

Throughout the devotional, you'll also find extra articles and activities to help you connect with the topic personally, such as Scripture memory verses, articles, and a list of resources.

day 1

IMPOSSIBLE JOY

___

discover |

At the start of this journey of learning to delight and find joy, spend some time in prayer. Ask God to reveal to you what true joy is.

It's easy to see that we live in a fallen, sinful world. Sickness, suffering, and sorrow surround us. Sometimes life becomes so difficult that finding joy seems impossible. These feelings can lead us to despair; to think our lives have no meaning. As Christians, it's even tempting to consider this life as something we just have to get through until we get to spend eternity with Jesus. But Jesus made it clear that God intended for us to do more than just exist.

READ
MATTHEW 6:33.

"But seek first the kingdom of God and his righteousness, and all these things will be provided for you."

He was instructing His listeners not to spend their lives focused on things of lesser concern, like food and clothing. Instead, Jesus taught them—and us—to focus on God first and to live life His way. When we seek God first, everything else falls into the right order. When we refuse to give in to worry, we can begin to see all the reasons we have to be joyful.

delight |

What did Jesus have to say about the purpose of our lives? Write it in your own words.

How do you seek God's kingdom first in your daily routine and activities?

How have you experienced joy by seeking God first in your life?

display |

Nothing God creates is meaningless. He created people on purpose, for purpose. Our lives should be focused on growing in our relationship with Him and building His kingdom on Earth. Our joy grows when we live out our purpose.

Think about your family, church, school, community, teams, clubs, and your group of friends. Where has God placed you? How can you model joy with these people in your life? How can you live focused on His purpose with these people? List at least two ideas you'll put into practice this week.

Are there situations in your life that feel pointless? Do you wonder how God could ever use them for His glory? Be honest with God about those situations. Ask Him to help you see how He is at work and to give you joy no matter what!

Use page 16 to help you memorize today's focus verse.

day 2

FAITH LEADS TO JOY

discover|

Even when we try to put God first and live for His kingdom, sorrow and sin remain active in the world. It's important for us to know how to persist in finding joy. When so much of life can seem overwhelming and outright depressing, it's important to know how to keep walking in joy no matter what's happening in our lives.

READ
1 PETER 1:8-9.

Though you have not seen him, you love him; though not seeing him now, you believe in him, and you rejoice with inexpressible and glorious joy, because you are receiving the goal of your faith, the salvation of your souls.

A major piece of finding joy is our faith in God, trusting who He is and the promises He has made to us. As Peter summarized in these verses: Even though we have never seen God with our eyes, we love and believe in Him. Through Jesus—because of the work of His death and resurrection—we can have life now and in eternity.

At the heart of being a Christian is trust in this reality. This trust allows us to celebrate what is and what will be with "inexpressible and glorious joy" (v. 8). Basically, faith is the key to sustaining joy in our lives.

delight |

How have you seen evidence that God is real and active in your life?

How has your faith helped you remain joyful?

> **As you continue to focus on the source of our joy, take a minute to thank God for giving you faith. Ask Him to increase your faith when life becomes difficult.**

display |

Faith nourishes joy. It's tough remain rooted in faith, but as we put God first in our lives and seek His kingdom above all else, we'll find our joy increasing.

The word *nourish* means to nurture, sustain, or grow. Grab three sticky notes or index cards. Make an artistic print on your computer or paper, with the words: nurture, grow, sustain, joy. Be as creative as you like. When you finish, place the art where you'll see it often. Ask God to show you all the ways you can nurture, grow, and sustain your joy.

Write out a short prayer of thanks for three things that bring you joy. Spend a minute recognizing that God gave you these things. Then, write out one way you can use each of those things to build the kingdom of God.

No Matter What

day 3

CERTAIN HOPE

___

discover|

We all have our "go to" products. Think about the one item you never leave home without. Maybe you have a favorite brand of chapstick or even a reusable water bottle that you love. When we truly love something, we want to tell our friends all about it, right? But the reality is, our favorite product might not work quite as well for them as it does for us. It might not turn out how we thought.

READ
ROMANS 15:7-13.

Now may the God of hope fill you with all joy and peace as you believe so that you may overflow with hope by the power of the Holy Spirit. —Romans 15:13

The hope described here is not the same as the desire for something to turn out the way we want—like our friends using the chapstick we recommend. Our hope in God is not based on chance or strong desires, but on certainty. We know this because of Jesus' life, death, burial, and resurrection. God permanently secured our hope through Jesus.

This hope is not something that may or may not work for us—God will always come through. God doesn't always work things out the way we want Him to, but things always happen just as He intends.

Hope from God is the source of overflowing joy for those who believe. As we put Him first and see His faithfulness, our relationship with God grows—and our faith and joy grow too.

delight |

There are many ways to grow in your relationship with God. Reading His Word, thinking deeply about it, and focusing your heart and mind on His truth are great ways to grow in your relationship with Him.

Name one way you've grown in your relationship with God in the last year.

How have you seen your joy increase as you've grown closer to God?

How have you seen God work on your behalf when you've needed Him?

display |

God often uses others to help us when we experience something difficult.

Write out the name of a person God used to help you through a difficult season. Text or call that person and let them know how God used them to help you.

> **Finding joy in your relationship with God requires you to actively seek Him. Spend some time in prayer, asking God grow your desire to know Him more each day.**

day 4

MADE TO WORSHIP

---

discover |

Think about the girls you know who just light up the room when they walk in. Or maybe it's the friend who can bring a smile to your face no matter what. Maybe you love being around her because she's funny, sweet, or encouraging. Whatever the reason, focus for a second on the feeling you have when you're in her presence. While you might truly enjoy time with that person, spending time with God can bring even greater joy.

READ
PSALM 16.

You reveal the path of life to me; in your presence is abundant joy; at your right hand are eternal pleasures. —Psalm 16:11

In today's passage, David—the author of Psalm 16—revealed his feelings toward God saying, "I have nothing good besides you" (v. 2), "LORD, you are my ... cup of blessing" (v. 5), and "I will always let the LORD guide me"(v. 8). These phrases indicate that spending time with God brought the deepest joy in David's life.

God's presence gives "abundant joy" (v. 11). Worship is one of the best ways to experience this type of closeness with God. You can worship God corporately when you gather with other believers. But worshiping God on your own is important too, when it's just you and God, and no one can see you. It's necessary to your spiritual health to experience both types of worship in your life.

delight |

We were made to worship. Anything we allow to consume our hearts and minds can be an object of worship. Sometimes we misdirect our worship to other things like sports, school, social media, and so on.

What are you worshiping?

How can you redirect your worship toward God?

When has worship brought you joy?

display |

Take a minute to worship God. Use a streaming service or search for a worship song in your personal music library that speaks to your heart and play it. Close your eyes, sing along, focus on the words, kneel, or lift your hands. Do whatever you feel led to do. No one is watching. Worship God and experience the joy of the Lord.

Write out the word *worship*. Use it to create an acrostic that describes how you feel about the Lord. Let these words serve as a time of joyful prayer to God for all He's done for you.

day 5

CHOOSE JOY

━━━━━

discover|

READ

PSALM 118.

This is the day the LORD has made; let's rejoice and be glad in it.
—Psalm 118:24

This Psalm describes a king's victorious return after battle. The psalmist made it clear that God won the battle—but the victory wasn't easy for them. He wrote about being in distress (v. 5), being hated (v. 7), surrounded (v. 10), and pushed (v. 13). In verse 18, he even talked about how severely the Lord disciplined him.

In spite of all of this, his praise in verse 24 is one of the most well known: "This is the day the Lord has made, let's rejoice and be glad in it!" He was distressed, hated, surrounded by his enemies, pushed and disciplined by God—and the psalmist still chose to delight in the Lord.

While we may not know what it's like to fight a physical battle, we do experience fight through difficult situations in our lives. Maybe we're the subject of the latest rumor, failed the last math test, experienced a tough breakup, or didn't get a part in the school play. No matter what we face, joy is a choice. Like the psalmist, we can choose joy, even in the midst of our biggest battles.

Take a minute to pray right now. Ask God to help you choose joy, no matter what circumstances you face. Write out your prayer in a journal or on a blank piece of paper.

delight |

We can rejoice even when we don't enjoy what we're facing. What we believe to be true about God will determine if we can choose joy, no matter what happens.

List five things you believe to be true about God. Search through your Bible to find out if what you believe about Him is true. (*Hint: Psalm 118 is a good place to begin your search.*)

Reflect on a circumstance you endured where God ultimately gave you victory. How did He sustain you as you walked through it? How did He give you joy even on the worst days?

display |

Use an app to create an image with the words from Psalm 118:24. Post the image on whatever social media platform you use. If anyone comments, choose joy as you respond. If you don't use social media, write it out on a sticky note and put it on your bathroom mirror. Memorize it and say it aloud any time you feel down.

If you are walking through a difficult time, go back to the prayer you just wrote. Keep it in a place where you won't forget it and return to it whenever you need to choose joy. Ask God for help when you need it.

"But seek first the kingdom of God and his righteousness,

AND ALL
THESE THINGS
WILL BE PROVIDED

OR YOU." MATTHEW 6:33

day 6

INTO THE UNKNOWN

discover |

Here's the deal: No one has life completely figured out. If you've started in wide-eyed wonder at the people who seem to have it all together—you're not alone. The good thing is, God knows we can't do life on our own. So, God—the very One who created the universe—promised to help.

READ

JOSHUA 1:6-9.

"Haven't I commanded you: be strong and courageous? Do not be afraid or discouraged, for the LORD your God is with you wherever you go." —Joshua 1:9

For 40 years, Moses led the Hebrews as they wandered in the wilderness on the edge of the promised land. When Moses died, the burden of leading the people fell to Joshua. In today's passage, God was encouraging Joshua and building him up for the task of conquering the land He'd promised to them. Talk about not having it all figured out. All Joshua had to go on was what God told him—and that was enough.

It's easy to think we might feel joy if we could just see the whole picture. But, sometimes, God shows us the way one step at a time. Joshua didn't know exactly what would happen as they entered the promised land, but he knew God was with him. He knew God had given them His law (the Ten Commandments) to follow. And he knew they would have success if he stayed on the path God had placed before him. Like Joshua, we trust God and take the next right step.

delight |

Real joy is not knowing everything that's in front of us; it's knowing God is with us as we go.

What unknown are you facing right now? How do God's words to Joshua give you hope?

Think about some difficult situations you've faced. How did your worry affect your thoughts and emotions? How did God walk with you during that time?

> **Life isn't like a movie or book where our circumstances end with the words, "And she lived happily ever after." But knowing God is with us makes a difference. Pray that you would be sensitive to God's presence with you as you navigate whatever difficulties you may be facing.**

display |

We experience joy in the unknown when we experience God. If we try to walk through the difficult days without Him, we won't experience joy along the way.

God took around 600 years to bring the Hebrews into the promised land. Just because you don't have what He's promised you today doesn't mean you never will. Instead of focusing on what you don't have, focus on what God has given you. Rejoice in that and write down three things He's done for you.

Seek out someone who is having a tough day. Just sit with them. You don't have to give them advice. Listen to them—maybe all they need is for someone to care.

day 7

WHAT IT TAKES

discover |

In life, we will all experience things that push us, things that make us wonder if we have what it takes to make it. While it can be super tempting to focus on the end goal—like making first chair, crossing the finish line, taking a bow as the curtains close—the truth is that anything worthwhile takes work. While it may sound a bit counterintuitive, finding joy takes work too.

READ
JAMES 1:2-4.

Consider it a great joy, my brothers and sisters, whenever you experience various trials, because you know that the testing of your faith produces endurance. And let endurance have its full effect, so that you may be mature and complete, lacking nothing.

All Christians will experience trying times throughout life, days when we want to give up, or feel like we just don't have what it takes. But like we play the same notes for hours on end, train every day for a 5K, or practice our lines a million times—finding joy means enduring the difficult days too. Christians must remember that trials are like the hours of preparation that will get us in the chair, across the finish line, or to the final bow.

Trials are never easy, but we ultimately know that Jesus helps us become mature and complete in all things. As we grow in faith, we learn that there can even be joy in the trials.

delight |

Think about something you had to work really hard to achieve. Whether it was for a project in school, an athletic event, or even something you made with your hands. What made all the hard work worth it?

Apply that same understanding to your faith. Spending time with God in worship, study of His Word, and prayer (among other things), brings us joy and helps us through those difficult circumstances. Reflect on a difficult season in your own life. Write about what God taught you and how He brought you joy.

display |

Even if you're a Christian, you might be thinking: "I just can't imagine joy at the end of what I'm going through." It's okay. Our faith sustains us, even when we're just not feeling very joyful.

Read Psalm 118:24. Now, consider this: *Joy is a choice.* We don't have to delight in our trials, but we delight in the God who is greater than our most difficult days.

Sometimes God allows us to experience a trial because it will help someone else who is walking through the same thing. Think about those around you. Ask God to reveal anyone around you who might benefit from hearing about your experience. Write out their names and commit to sharing your story with them this week. Remember, the point is not to tell how *you* overcame, but to point them to God and how He helped you overcome.

Pray a bold prayer today. Ask God to use the trials you endure to make you mature and complete so that you will lack nothing.

No Matter What

day 8

discover

The early church faced a controversial question: What was right for a believer to eat? This may not seem like a big deal to you, but this question was rooted in the Jewish beliefs still held by many of the first Christians. Jews had very specific laws about their diet, so when they became Christians, they had a tough time walking away from their old ways of thinking. They needed to learn that joy was not found in judging what their fellow believers did or didn't eat. Real joy came from somewhere else.

READ

ROMANS 14:13-23.

Therefore, do not let your good be slandered, for the kingdom of God is not eating and drinking, but righteousness, peace, and joy in the Holy Spirit. Whoever serves Christ in this way is acceptable to God and receives human approval.
—Romans 14:16-18

This type of thinking still exists in churches today, but it looks different. Instead of judging someone for what they do or don't eat, believers might criticize others for how they look or because they hold a different opinion from our own. Truthfully, it's difficult not to live in this space, but we'll never find joy living in judgment.

Jesus didn't build His church on appearances; He built His church on what happens on the inside, in our hearts. The Holy Spirit is the One who helps shape us and mold us in righteousness, peace, and joy. So, real joy doesn't come from looking the part on the outside, but by letting the Lord change us from the inside out.

It's so tempting to just try to look the part, but that won't last. Eventually what's really on the inside will emerge and become evident to those around us.

> **Ask God to shape you from the inside out and to keep you from judging others by their outward appearance.**

delight |

To be changed on the inside, we must look at our own hearts and ask ourselves some tough questions. Take a few minutes and ask yourself:

Where have I been guilty of judging others and thinking it will make me feel good about myself?

What attitudes need to change in my own heart so that I can experience the righteousness, peace, and joy described in verse 17?

display |

When we seek to be changed from within by the Holy Spirit, we gain the approval of both God and people (v. 18). This means our motives are revealed to be pure in all that we do. Does this describe you? Why or why not?

Examine your heart and see if the good you seek to do is from a pure motive. If it's not, confess to God and repent of any impure motives.

Do something good for someone else quietly, without taking credit. Pray that God would give you more opportunities to love others well even when you won't be recognized for doing good.

day 9

███████████▏

discover |

Think back to a time when you got a good grade on a test or project. Remember how good it felt to show your parents the grade or casually mention your score to your friends (getting your humblebrag on)? Even thinking back on the experience might make you feel good inside but the initial rush wears off over time. Ultimately, the good feeling of the moment does not amount to real, lasting joy.

READ

LUKE 15:8-10.

"I tell you, in the same way, there is joy in the presence of God's angels over one sinner who repents." —Luke 15:10

In this parable, the coin the woman lost was worth about what someone would get paid for a day of work.[2] This wasn't overkill; it wasn't like turning the house over for a penny. Her diligence to find it revealed she wasn't a person of great means. She needed that coin to live, so when she found the coin, she wanted to tell everyone she knew.

The point of the parable is that each person is of infinite value and worth to God. When someone comes to faith in Jesus, it's not just a passing thing that wears off over time. It means someone has moved from death to life. This lasting celebration is what real joy looks like.

> For today, the Delight section of the devotion will be an extended time of prayer. Take a minute to prepare your heart to spend some time in an attitude and posture of prayer.

delight |

He loves you so much that He sent His only Son to die for you. Take a moment and reflect on how much God loves and values you.

Thank Jesus that He willingly gave His life so that you could live.

Who were the people in your life that diligently poured into you, witnessed to you, and loved you until you God rescued you? Thank God for those people and their desire to see you come to faith in Christ.

display |

Pure joy comes when someone repents of sin and turns to Christ—this is the kind of joy that lasts forever.

Who do you know that doesn't know Jesus? Think about the joy you would feel if they trusted Him as Savior. Think about the eternal joy they would feel giving their lives to Christ. What can you do to introduce them to Jesus or have a deeper conversation about their faith?

True joy is found in Jesus. Is that evident by the life you lead? What can do that reveals this truth in your life? How can you make this joy more evident to those around you?

No Matter What

day 10

discover

It's easy to look at our lives and think nothing will ever change; that things just are the way they are and there's nothing we can do about it. That sounds depressing, right? But the truth is that all people will experience the same outcome. Unless the Lord returns first, everyone will die. No matter what our circumstances are right now, we have a choice to make the most of it for God's glory.

READ

ECCLESIASTES 9:1-6.

But there is hope for whoever is joined with all the living, since a live dog is better than a dead lion. For the living know that they will die, but the dead don't know anything. There is no longer a reward for them because the memory of them is forgotten. —Ecclesiastes 9:4-5

Simply put: When you're alive, you have a choice in how you live; you don't when you're dead. A lion may be mightier and more majestic than a dog, but a live dog is better than a dead lion. Christians know we won't live here forever—when our time has come, we will be with the Lord. Until then, we choose to live for Him, seeking His kingdom and righteousness first.

But those who choose not to trust in Jesus as Savior, don't realize that they won't have another chance. When this life is over, they won't have another opportunity to make a different choice about how they live. At that point their choice will have been made.

delight |

This truth can lead you two respond in two ways: You may feel sad or depressed because people who don't know the Lord can't experience the joy He has for them here and in eternity. Or you may be inspired by the truth to share this good news and joy with those around you.

Understanding that our time on earth is limited, take an inventory of your life. How are you spending your time? Are you giving your life to things that matter in eternity or to things that will fade away?

Think of the people you know who haven't yet chosen to follow God. How might you be able to share with them the hope and joy that only come from God?

> **Talk to God about how you are spending your time. If you are not using it for Him and His glory, repent of that and ask God to help you live your life completely surrendered to Him. Thank God for directing your path.**

display |

This ends the section on *What Real Joy Looks Like*. Consider the last five days of devotions as you respond to the following:

What's one new insight you gained about joy?

Are you seeking and choosing joy? Or are you stuck in feelings of despair? If you're feeling down, ask God to show you the way out.

how blue are you?

Everyone feels a little blue. But how do you know when you've moved from feeling down to outright depression? While this page is not meant to act as a diagnostic test, you'll find some questions to help you determine your level of depression. Use a blue highlighter to select the answer that best describes you.

1 I feel hopeless about pretty much everything.
Nope.   Eh, maybe.   Sometimes.   Definitely.

2 I'm tired most of the time, but I don't know why.
Nope.   Eh, maybe.   Sometimes.   Definitely.

3 I have felt really down; not even things or people I love can cheer me up.
Nope.   Eh, maybe.   Sometimes.   Definitely.

4 I haven't really wanted to do anything. Moving takes too much effort.
Nope.   Eh, maybe.   Sometimes.   Definitely.

5 I don't fall asleep easily, and I don't sleep well once I do.
Nope.   Eh, maybe.   Sometimes.   Definitely.

6 Most days, I'd love to just stay in bed and do nothing.
Nope.   Eh, maybe.   Sometimes.   Definitely.

7 I struggle to feel joyful.
Nope.   Eh, maybe.   Sometimes.   Definitely.

8 I'm incredibly indecisive.
Nope.   Eh, maybe.   Sometimes.   Definitely.

9 I usually feel upset and can't sit still.
Nope.   Eh, maybe.   Sometimes.   Definitely.

10 At times, I've wondered if life is worth living.
Nope.   Eh, maybe.   Sometimes.   Definitely.

Every "Eh, maybe" answer is worth 1 point. Every "Sometimes" answer is worth 3 points, and every "Definitely" highlighted is worth 5 points. Total: _____.

These numbers indicate what your depression level is *likely* to be. 0-15 is low, 16-30 is moderate, and 31-50 is high. If you're feeling depressed at all, it would be a good idea to talk with your parents about meeting with your pastor, a certified Christian counselor, or your doctor for a personalized and professional assessment.[5]

what can i do when i'm feeling down?

While those who struggle with depression should seek professional help, here are some practical tips to add a little joy to even the worst of days.

1 Spend time with the people you love. Sometimes, we just need someone to be there, to listen, or inspire us to move when we're down.

2 Take care of yourself. Getting enough sleep, eating foods that are good for you, drinking enough water, and exercising also help boost your mood.

3 Get outside. Maybe you're an avid hiker or dancer, or maybe you enjoy walking through a beautiful garden, or maybe you'd rather watch the sun set over the lake. No matter your preference, spending time outside is good for your brain and your body!

4 Counter every lie with a positive truth. We all believe lies about ourselves, but God's Word is filled with the truth. And when we can't see our way to the light, family and friends can be a huge help! For every lie or negative thought that pops into your head, write out a truth. Consider keeping a journal specifically for this purpose.

5 Laugh. Right now, you may feel down, but you will experience joy again (Ps. 30:5). Watch a funny movie, TV show, or video online. Or consider finding videos of a comedian like Tim Hawkins, Chonda Pierce, or Michael Jr. You might also enjoy Beth Moore's "The Donk Chronicles" videos about her friendship with an adorable donkey next door.

6 Get creative. If you enjoy painting, singing, drawing, crafting, graphic design, photography, or any other creative activity, make time to do it.

What are some other ways you can create space for joy in your life?

This is neither an exhaustive list or therapeutic advice. For specific help in your own struggle, talk with a mental health professional.

day 11

SOMETHING'S NOT RIGHT

discover |

A recent study showed that 20 percent of girls ages 12-17 have suffered from depression within the last year. And young people generally worry about anxiety and depression among their peers.[3] So if you've ever felt depressed, you're certainly not alone. Depression is a common issue for countless people—particularly girls—but the good news is that God can help us fight it.

READ
ROMANS 8:22-25.

For we know that the whole creation has been groaning together with labor pains until now. Not only that, but we ourselves who have the Spirit as the firstfruits—we also groan within ourselves, eagerly waiting for adoption, the redemption of our bodies. —Romans 8:22-23

The word *groaning* points to an internal, inaudible prayer, typically filled with grief.[4] All of creation cries out with this grief, which comes from sin. When sin entered the world (Gen. 3), God's perfect design was distorted from its original intent. So, things like sickness, natural disasters, and all kinds of suffering—including depression—became a part of life on earth. But the greatest consequence of sin is death.

Sometimes our personal sin does cause depression (we'll deal with that on Day 14), but depression is not always a result of sins we've committed. Depression can be biological, circumstantial, or genetic. It can even be a result of someone else's sin. No matter what the cause of depression, it's important to understand this key truth: Depression exists because sin exists.

delight |

Depression occurs because sin has tainted God's perfect creation. If there was no sin, then there would be no depression.

If you're suffering from depression, take a second to recognize that it does not come from God. God loves us and doesn't want us to be depressed.

> **We know God loves us and doesn't want us to be depressed; He wants us to be filled with joy. We can be confident of this truth because He sent Jesus to die for us. Dwell on this truth. We have a chance at life because of Jesus.**

display |

Depression is a reality for many people today, even Christians; it doesn't magically go away just because you're a Christian. As verse 23 reminds us, even those of us with the Spirit "groan inwardly." But, we also know God offers hope.

If you are struggling with depression, find help. If this seems intimidating, first talk to a trusted adult—your parents, your youth pastor, or a mentor. If you need to meet with a professional counselor or therapist, please don't hesitate. You don't have to—and shouldn't—face your struggle with depression on your own. Take a look at the Resources on pages 48-49 for more information.

List three verses we've read so far that have encouraged you. If you're not struggling with depression or feeling discouraged, then share them someone who is.

Listen to the song "Confident" by Steffany Gretzinger (*Blackout*, 2018). Consider singing along as a prayer of praise and confidence in God's goodness.

day 12

discover|

So much of what we find on the news or even on social media is negative. We're surrounded by numerous tragedies and terrible things. But what we experience from a distance doesn't even speak to the difficult things we go through on a personal level. It's no wonder so many of us feel depressed and struggle to find joy.

READ
PSALM 94.

If I say, "My foot is slipping," your faithful love will support me, LORD. When I am filled with cares, your comfort brings me joy. —Psalm 94:18-19

The psalmist was no stranger to tragedy. This psalm speaks of wicked people who killed widows, foreigners, and orphans (v. 6). How do you respond to something like that? The overwhelming oppression caused the people to ask: Where is God? But the psalmist reminded them that God will never leave His people—and we can take comfort in this truth too (v. 14). Even when we are filled with worry, anxiety, or depression, God's love brings us joy.

Here's the truth: Some people are depressed because they've experienced awful things. Focusing on God's love won't automatically cure depression and give joy, but it teaches your mind to focus on the good that comes from the Lord. Focusing on all that's gone wrong only strengthens negative thought patterns. Walking in deeper joy means looking at the depth of God's love rather than the depth of our pain.

delight |

What's one choice you can make to walk in deeper joy today?

How can you turn your attention away from the tragedies and difficulties you've faced in life and toward God's love and the joy He can provide?

display |

Difficult circumstances can contribute to depression. You might even know someone who's dealing with something difficult and feeling pretty down or depressed.

If you have a friend in this situation, write her name on an index card or sticky note. Place the note in your Bible. Then, whenever you come across that name, pause and pray for her.

Pray about reaching out to your friend, too. You don't have to give advice or try to make her feel better. Call, go, video chat, text. Be present and listen.

Focus your attention on God and His love. As a prayer exercise, write out anything about God's love that comes to mind. If you need more room to write, grab a sheet of paper or notebook. Then pray back through that list, thanking God for His love and letting that lead your thoughts.

day 13

A REAL ENEMY

discover|

READ
1 PETER 5:6-9.

Humble yourselves, therefore, under the mighty hand of God, so that he may exalt you at the proper time, casting all your cares on him, because he cares about you. —1 Peter 5:6-7

Our enemy, Satan, will do anything to keep people trapped in depression. His goal is to devour. He wants to rip away our joy and make our lives miserable. Like a lion, he patiently waits for the right moment, then attacks and consumes. Peter offers four ways we can defend ourselves from his attacks:

- Humble yourselves (v. 6).

- Cast your cares on God (v. 7).

- Be sober-minded and alert (v. 8).

- Resist (v. 9).

Satan attacks every believer around the world (v. 9). While we don't want others to hurt, it's encouraging to know we're not alone. We stand against the enemy with our brothers and sisters in Christ. We help one another face the temptation to live in discouragement and depression.

It's also good to remember God cares for us (v. 7). God didn't command these four actions to make life more difficult. He did it so we can experience joy and freedom from the enemy's schemes. We don't act out of obligation. We act because we need God desperately, and because He's proven His love to us over and over.

delight |

Think about these four actions. Name one way you can do each of them to delight in the Lord and embrace joy.

- Humble yourself:

- Cast your cares on God:

- Be sober-minded and alert:

- Resist:

> **Now go back over what you wrote and restate each one as a prayer. You can structure your prayer like this:** *Lord, help me to humble myself by...*

display |

Our God is stronger than our enemy. The Spirit that lives in us is greater than the one who lives in the world (1 John 4:4).

How can you strengthen your defenses against the enemy? List three ideas to help you live in joy rather than despair.

Name two other godly girls who are walking with you and fighting alongside you against the enemy. Thank God for them today.

On an index card or sticky note write out the words *God loves me.* Be as creative and artsy as you want! Put the note somewhere you'll see it often.

day 14

JOY RESTORED

discover|

Remember people can be depressed because …

- sin has tainted God's original design for the world and the people in it.
- truly terrible things happen to and around us.
- our enemy wants to devour us and leave us in despair.

But let's take a look at another reason we might feel depressed.

READ
PSALM 51:1-13.

God, create a clean heart for me and renew a steadfast spirit within me. Do not banish me from your presence or take your Holy Spirit from me. Restore the joy of your salvation to me, and sustain me by giving me a willing spirit.
—Psalm 51:10-12

In this Psalm, David cried out for forgiveness for adultery and murder. The prophet Nathan had confronted David, and David immediately felt convicted of his sin. As a result of his sinful decisions, David experienced a season of despair (v. 8). This psalm was David's prayer of repentance and asking God to deliver him.

Our lack of joy is sometimes caused by our own sinfulness too. Maybe a habit or a secret sin isolates us from God and others, and we feel alone and depressed because of it. All of us have sinned. But the good news is that God offers forgiveness to all of us too. How we choose to respond to our sin determines how quickly we being our journey out of despair and into joy.

delight |

David asked God to give him a clean heart (v. 10). When have you asked God to do the same for you?

Asking God for a clean heart means giving Him complete control of—and access to—even the places we try to keep hidden in our hearts. What might it look like for you to give Him control over and access to your whole heart?

display |

Once God restored David and put him on the right path, David still had to live with the consequences of his choices. This didn't mean David didn't have God's love and forgiveness. But forgiveness doesn't mean the consequences of our sins vanish.

If you've sinned against someone else and God has revealed this to you, what will you do to try to restore the relationship?

Sometimes confession is the first step toward joy. If the Holy Spirit has convicted you of sin in your life that you need to confess, take the time to do so now.

The LORD is my shepherd;

I HAVE WHAT I NEED.

He lets me lie down in green pastures;
he leads me beside quiet waters.

HE RENEWS MY LIFE;

he leads me along the right paths
for his name's sake.

EVEN WHEN I GO THROUGH THE

DARKEST VALLEY, I FEAR NO DANGER,

FOR YOU ARE WITH ME;

your rod and your staff
they comfort me.

YOU PREPARE A TABLE BEFORE ME

IN THE PRESENCE OF MY ENEMIES;

you anoint my head with oil;

MY CUP OVERFLOWS.

Only goodness and faithful love
will pursue me all the days of my life,

AND I WILL DWELL IN THE

HOUSE OF THE LORD AS

LONG AS I LIVE.

PSALM 23

day 15

discover |

Unfortunately, there is a stigma surrounding mental health in the Christian community. People sometimes think those who are depressed must have done something wrong or maybe their faith just isn't strong enough. While sin can sometimes be the source of depression, it isn't always. Sometimes circumstances, brain chemistry, or even someone else's sin toward us triggers depression in us.

READ

PSALM 23.

Even when I go through the darkest valley, I fear no danger, for you are with me; your rod and your staff—they comfort me. —Psalm 23:4

David had his fair share of dark, depressing days. And many of those difficult days were the result of someone else's actions. In verse 4, David wrote about going "through the darkest valley." This valley might have been when he was in physical danger or mental anguish, or it could have been the result of emotional trauma. Whatever the circumstance, David knew God was with him even in that "darkest valley." He knew that the Lord was still protecting him like a shepherd protects his sheep.

Depression can be like a dark valley, and some of us may find ourselves walking right through the middle of it. If you do find yourself in that dark valley, know that God is there with you. He promises that He will never, ever leave or forsake you (Deut. 31:6).

delight |

Psalm 23 is a picture of a shepherd (God) and His sheep (us). The job of a shepherd is to watch over sheep who tend to wander off to dangerous places. This is the nature of our relationship with God too. He watches over us and protects us.

Think about the dark valleys you've walked through. How did God remind you of His presence, even there?

God is there for you—no matter where you are. How can you trust Him to comfort you, lead you, protect you, and walk with you through any valley?

display |

One of the best protections for us as we walk through valleys is God's Word. Knowing Scripture can help you defend yourself from the enemy's attacks and can rescue you from dangerous places.

Use pages 38-39 to work on memorizing Psalm 23.

Take a moment and summarize Psalm 23 in your own words. Focus on the truth of the Scripture, and be confident that God walks with you trust Him fully.

Praise God for His presence. Let the words to this psalm, a favorite praise song, or hymn guide the words of your prayer.

day 16

MENDING A BROKEN HEART

discover |

Have you ever had a broken heart? Have you ever felt crushed inside? No one likes or wants to experience these feelings, but we've probably all felt like this from time to time. We feel this way because we're human—we aren't unbreakable physically or emotionally. People gossip. We experience rejection. Friends lie. Thankfully, God Himself gives hope for the brokenhearted.

READ PSALM 34.

The LORD is near the brokenhearted; he saves those crushed in spirit.
—Psalm 34:18

David wrote this psalm during one of the most difficult seasons in his life; he was crushed. He was on the run from King Saul because God had chosen David to be the new King of Israel instead of Saul. Saul wasn't very interested in giving up his throne, so he wanted to kill David. David fled to a place called Gath. When he arrived, he pretended to be insane to protect himself.

But look at the words David wrote in response to this experience: "I will bless the LORD" (v. 1), "boast in the LORD" (v. 2), and "proclaim the LORD's greatness" (v. 3). You might be wondering how a man who thought his only chance at survival was faking insanity could still praise God. Here's the thing: David's relationship with God ran deeper than his fear and feelings. He *knew* God was near, even when he felt brokenhearted and crushed.

delight |

As a verb, the word *delight* means to please someone greatly. As a noun it means great pleasure.[6]

How do you take delight in the Lord when you feel brokenhearted and crushed?

How can you bring delight to the Lord, even when you feel brokenhearted and crushed?

> **Ask God to help you know in your heart that He is good and He is near when you are heartbroken. Use Psalm 34 as a prayer. If you find that parts of it are difficult to pray, turn David's proclamation of faith into a request for deeper trust in the Lord's goodness.**

display |

We know that we'll face heartbreak in life. Having an idea of how you'll approach difficult days might help you walk through them without giving in to despair.

Write out the words *God is close to the brokenhearted. Therefore I will…* Then list five things you plan to do the next time you experience heartbreak.

If you are feeling down today, then write out Psalm 34:18 on a note card. Fold the card and put it in your pocket. If sadness threatens to overwhelm you, take out the note, read it, and be reminded that the Lord is closer than you can imagine.

day 17

JUST BE THERE

discover |

If someone asked you what a fish looks like, you probably wouldn't have any difficulty answering that question. A fish lives in water, has fins and gills, eyes on the sides of its head, and can be a variety of colors. But when someone asks what a Christian looks like, the answer might not come so easily. Thankfully, several places in the Bible describe what Christians should look like.

READ
ROMANS 12:9-16.

Rejoice with those who rejoice; weep with those who weep.
—Romans 12:15

This passage is full of do's and don'ts for Christ followers. The character traits on this list should be words that people would use to describe us.

Christians should "Rejoice in hope; be patient in affliction; be persistent in prayer" (v. 12). But we should also take time to weep with those who weep. God calls us to be empathetic people— attempting to understand how others feel. God calls us to pause and care for others. God calls us to listen to those who are hurting. God calls us to be there for those who are struggling to find joy.

delight |

We can become empathetic people. We can try to think about how we would feel in their situation. We can try to be good friends. Sometimes, just being there and listening is the best thing you can do.

An important verse to remember to help us be empathetic is the shortest verse in the Bible: "Jesus wept" (John 11:35). Jesus was human just like us. He felt pain and sorrow with and for others. We are called to do the same. What do you need to do in your own heart to be more available to weep with others?

It's not always easy to be there for others. Pray that God would move in your heart to make you more empathetic. Ask Him to give you opportunities to simply be there for someone else.

display |

Sometimes people stay stuck in depression because no one bothers to reach out to them and weep with them. No one is there for them.

Have you taken time out of your life to just pause and listen to someone? If you haven't lately, here's a challenge for you. Text a friend you know who might be hurting. Arrange a time to sit down with them and just talk. When you get there, put away your phone or anything that might distract you, give them your full attention, and just listen.

Create an acrostic of the word *empathy*. For each letter, write out one way you can be empathetic toward the people around you—even those who are tough to get along with.

No Matter What

day 18

WEAKNESS > STRENGTH

discover |

Time and again, God's Word reveals that God is near the brokenhearted and calls us to be there for those who are struggling. But God could be working through depression in ways we never imagined.

READ
2 CORINTHIANS 12:1-10.

But he said to me, "My grace is sufficient for you, for my power is perfected in weakness." Therefore, I will most gladly boast all the more about my weaknesses, so that Christ's power may reside in me. So I take pleasure in weaknesses, insults, hardships, persecutions, and in difficulties, for the sake of Christ. For when I am weak, then I am strong. —2 Corinthians 12:9-10

God used the Apostle Paul to do great things. During his ministry, Paul planted churches, wrote much of the New Testament, and shared the gospel with too many people to count. If anyone would be perceived as strong, it would be Paul. But in these verses, Paul was bragging about his weaknesses. When we know we can't do something on our own, we're more likely to ask for help—and we're more likely to lean on God.

God gave Paul a built in weakness so that he would rely on the Lord (v. 7). God can use even depression to bring us closer to Him and help us learn to rely on Him completely. When you struggle, when you feel like you can't take another step, stop and think of how God might be working through you in this situation.

delight |

Let's be clear: God doesn't want us to be depressed, and He doesn't give us depression. But we need to know God is so big and mighty that He can use something bad—like depression—for good in the long run.

Read Romans 8:28. How can God use the negative and discouraging things in life for His glory and our good?

Read Psalm 30:11. What has to happen in your life for you to be able to joyfully proclaim these verses from your own heart?

display |

One of the ways God turns our weakness into His strength is by giving us opportunities to use our experiences to speak truth and hope into others' lives.

What have you endured that you might be able to share with others to help them walk through difficult days?

Who walked with you through your difficult days? Name one person who was there for you. Consider texting that person today to tell them thank you.

> **Ask God to help you see how what you've been through might help someone else. Then, thank God for that person (or people) who walked with you through your trial.**

resources

books

- *Unshakable Hope* by Max Lucado

- *What to Do When You Don't Know What to Do: Discouragement and Depression* by Henry Cloud and John Townsend

- *Get Out of Your Head* by Jennie Allen

- *You are Free* by Rebekah Lyons

- *Get Out of that Pit* by Beth Moore

articles

- "Why Christian Love Matters in Depression" by Kathryn Butler (The Gospel Coalition, 2018)

- "8 ways to help depressed Christians" by David Murray (The Ethics and Religious Liberty Commission [ERLC], 2017)

- "How the church can be a community to those with depression" by Garrick D. Conner (ERLC, 2019)

videos and podcasts

- "Finding Joy - Coffee with Chrystal #alittleQC" by Chrystal Evans Hurst (Youtube)

- "How Should We Respond to Suffering? | Kelly Minter" by LifeWay Christian Resources (Youtube)

- "How does the gospel speak hope in the battle with depression?" by Jennifer Michelle Greenburg (ERLC)

find a counselor

Always, always talk with your parents if you're struggling. If you want to talk to a counselor or if your parents have approached you about doing so, these tools can help.

This list is certainly not exhaustive, but you and your parents can do the following to help you find a solid, biblical counselor.

- Check with your church first to see if they have qualified counselors on-site or have a list of recommended counselors to refer you to.
- Use a reputable search site to find a Christian Counselor near you. These sites provide a search-by-location feature, but it's still a good idea to go through your results and make sure the counselor has experience with depression. These two sites are good places to start.
  - The Christian Counselor's Network (powered by Focus on the Family)
  - Christian Care Connect (powered by the American Association of Christian Counselors)

in case of emergency

Sometimes depression roots itself deep inside and causes suicidal thoughts. If you're experiencing any of these thoughts, please reach out now. Even if you aren't experiencing these thoughts, you may know someone who is. Here are some people you can contact if you need help.

- If you have a counselor, contact them immediately. Most counselors have an emergency line for off-hours.
- National Suicide Prevention Lifeline. Call 1-800-273-8255 or chat on their website at https://suicidepreventionlifeline.org.
- New Hope Telephone Counseling Center. Call 714-639-4673 to connect with a trained crisis prevention specialist.
- National Alliance on Mental Illness. Call 1-800-950-6264.
- To Write Love on Her Arms. Text TWLOHA to 741741 for their crises text line, and check out their resources page here: https://twloha.com/find-help/. On this page you'll find links to 24-hour hotlines and other helps.

day 19

discover |

When we talk about Scripture and faith as part of overcoming depression, this doesn't discount the fact that we might need medication and counseling too. God created each one of us uniquely, and He provides various tools to help us overcome depression. But Scripture is key because it draws us closer to God, changing us and the way we think. Our mindset about joy is an important and necessary element in overcoming despair in our lives. It helps us to manage, and sometimes overcome, depression.

READ
PHILIPPIANS 4:4-8.

Finally brothers and sisters, whatever is true, whatever is honorable, whatever is just, whatever is pure, whatever is lovely, whatever is commendable— if there is any moral excellence and if there is anything praiseworthy— dwell on these things. —Philippians 4:8

Have you ever wanted something so much that it consumed your thoughts? You started seeing it everywhere you look, and you noticed other people who had it. Maybe you felt borderline obsessed with it. This is what it means to dwell on something.

In today's passage, the Apostle Paul instructed us to dwell on certain things that bring joy. To simply believe that these things are good doesn't get you where you need to be. If we want to have joy in our lives and fight against depression, then we have to dwell on good things.

delight |

When Paul instructed us to "rejoice in the Lord" (v. 4), he wrote from a prison cell. He knew what it was like to live through difficult days, and still he rejoiced.

Think about the list Paul wrote in verse 8. Which people in your life mirror these qualities? List one beside each of the following.

- Truthfulness:
- Honor:
- Justice:
- Purity:
- Loveliness:
- Being commendable (admirable):
- Moral Excellence:

display |

Ask yourself these questions to help you consider how you might display to others that you're focusing on joyful things.

How do my words bring joy? Which words need to be added and deleted from my vocabulary to bring more joy to my life?

How do my actions bring joy? Which actions need to be added and deleted from my daily activities to bring more joy to my days?

It takes real effort to focus on joyful things. Spend some time talking to God about where your mind usually wanders. Ask Him to direct your thoughts and help you dwell on Him and things that are good.

day 20

discover|

On a TV show called *Alone*, survival experts are dropped in remote places, and they try to live with only a few survival tools all by themselves. The winners often stay weeks in hostile places, talking to themselves and eating gross things (like squirrels and bugs) just to survive. That sounds terrifying, right?

For a moment, Joshua thought he would be alone. Technically, he would never be by himself like the people on *Alone*, but he would be without his leader. For years, Moses led the Hebrews—from slavery in Egypt to freedom and the edge of the promised land. His time as leader was ending and Joshua would be taking over.

READ

DEUTERONOMY 31:1-8.

"The LORD is the one who will go before you. He will be with you; he will not leave you or abandon you. Do not be afraid or discouraged." —Deuteronomy 31:8

Even though Joshua wouldn't have Moses as they crossed the Jordan River and entered the promised land, he had someone better. God would not just go with Joshua, He would go before him. God would be the One who would take care of the people. God would be the One who would drive out their enemies. By no means would Joshua be alone; the Lord Almighty was with him.

Take a moment and reflect on this truth. God is with you. He goes before you. Thank Him for doing this. Write out specific moments when you could feel His presence with you.

delight |

When have you felt alone, even though you knew deep down that God was with you?

What are some ways you can actively remind yourself that God is with you?

How has God proven to you over the course of your life that you are not alone?

How has God "gone before you"?

display |

Think about your friends. Who might feel alone right now? List any names that come to mind. Consider some ways you can connect with them more often and on a deeper level. Jot down a few ideas.

When you're tempted to tell yourself that you're alone, try speaking aloud the words: *God goes before me. I am never alone.*

day 21

discover |

About 600 years before Jesus was born, there was a prophet named Habakkuk. During his lifetime, the Jewish people were under siege from the Babylonians. Eventually, they would fall to Babylon and be exiled from Jerusalem. Imagine being taken from your home and forced to live in another country.

READ
HABAKKUK 3:16-19.

Though the fig tree does not bud and there is no fruit on the vines, though the olive crop fails and the fields produce no food, though the flocks disappear from the pen and there are no herds in the stalls, yet I will celebrate in the LORD; I will rejoice in the God of my salvation!
—Habakkuk 3:17-18

There's no other way to say it: Life for the Jews was terrible during these years. Habakkuk illustrated their situation poetically by comparing it to trees that didn't bloom, fields that didn't yield crops, and animals who disappeared from their pastures. In spite of all their difficulties and despair, Habakkuk still found joy in the Lord because of his salvation.

Maybe you get it; you totally identify with Habakkuk. You might feel like nothing is going right for you at the moment. But, like Habakkuk, you can experience joy—no matter what—by remembering your salvation.

delight |

If you've trusted in Jesus as your Savior and Lord, consider recording your testimony and sharing it with friends who need to hear the gospel.

If you haven't experienced salvation, talk with your parents, a trusted Christian mentor, or your student pastor about what it means to place your faith in Jesus.

> **Read Romans 8:38-39 aloud as a prayer. With boldness and confidence, praise the Lord that nothing—no matter how bad it may seem— can separate you from His love.**

display |

Repetition helps us remember. So, repeat to yourself the end of Habakkuk 3:18 today: "I will rejoice in the God of my salvation!"

Think about your life. Write out one difficult thing you experienced in the past and one difficult thing you're experiencing now. Then, beside each thing, write the phrase, *I will rejoice in the God of my salvation.*

Write your own poem or song, expressing specific ways you've felt joy in the Lord even when nothing seemed to be going right.

No Matter What

day 22

STILL HERE

discover

We need strong leaders. They give us clear direction, wisdom, and encouragement. Without leaders, it's difficult to know the right way to go and many of our most important questions remain unanswered. When leaders tell us what to do, it's for our good—the best leaders want what's best for the people under their care.

READ
ISAIAH 41:8-16.

Do not fear, for I am with you; do not be afraid, for I am your God.
I will strengthen you; I will help you;
I will hold on to you with my righteous right hand.
—Isaiah 41:10

God is our ultimate leader. We can see how He encouraged and gave direction to His people, despite the fact that they were in this situation because of their own disobedience. They were about to be conquered by Babylon.

Essentially, God said, "Yes, I know you're scared. But I am still God. I am still here. Don't be afraid; I've got you." Even though the Israelites had disobeyed and drifted, they were still His people—and He dearly loved them.

God's people would have to face the results of their sin, but their sin wouldn't have the last word. Just as God led the Israelites with a command to not be afraid, He says the same thing to us. We just have to choose to trust Him and trust that He will be our strength, our help, and the One who holds us up.

> Are there places in your life where you know your actions or words
> have caused your trouble? If so, ask the Lord to help you turn away
> from those things. When we live in those sins, it's often more difficult
> to remember God is with us.

delight |

There are times in our lives when, like Israel, we cause our own distress. That doesn't mean God is finished with us. He is still there, showing us the way.

It's impossible to experience God's joy while living in sin. In what areas of your life are you holding onto sin while also reaching for God's joy?

It's also important to remember that when we do sin, God doesn't discard us forever. If you are dealing with the aftermath of your sin, take a minute to ask God to help you handle it with grace, but to learn what you can from it so that you can move forward in joy.

display |

Israel's rejection of the Lord meant they had to live in exile for a time, but it didn't mean they were no longer His people. God still had a plan for them, which was ultimately fulfilled in Jesus.

Get creative: Write, hand letter, or design a print of this phrase: *My sin does not have the last word—God does.* Because God has the final say over us, we can repent and live in faith instead of fear, knowing He is with us. Place the phrase where you'll see it often.

day 23

WHAT COMES NEXT?

discover |

Countless movies are written to leave us hanging, waiting for a sequel—as long as it's successful. For the movie-makers, a sequel means more money. But most people like sequels because they want to know the rest of the story for the characters they've fallen in love with.

As we discovered yesterday, our sin causes us pain. But, even then, God is still with us and for us. Now, let's take a look at the rest of the story.

READ
PSALM 30.

For his anger lasts only a moment, but his favor, a lifetime. Weeping may stay overnight, but there is joy in the morning.
—Psalm 30:5

Here's the truth: God hates sin. Sin brought brokenness into His world and into His people—a people He sent His own Son to die for. But when we repent and turn from our sins, there is joy. The psalmist explained this well by telling us: "his anger lasts only a moment, but his favor, a lifetime" (v. 5).

Like the poet Alexander Pope said, "hope springs eternal."[7] This phrase is exactly what we have in God. Every day our hope is renewed. We may feel down or hurt for a season, but joy will always be there too. Every day our hope springs up again. Just like a good sequel, God's story with us doesn't end with His anger over our sin—instead, it continues in the joy that comes from our repentance and His forgiveness.

delight |

At times, we might be tempted to give in to sin because we know God will forgive us. When we do this, we cheapen the sacrifice Jesus made for sin. This is not an attitude of repentance or joy.

When have you felt tempted to give in to sin, knowing God would forgive you?

We cheapen God's grace when we willfully disobey Him, knowing His forgiveness awaits us on the other side. How can you avoid this way of thinking?

Pray that God will help you avoid the trap of willful disobedience. Ask Him to remind you of the joy He brings and to help you live in that rather than experiencing the pain of sin.

display |

Remember that God is for you, not against you. He wants you to experience joy, and there's no joy in sin. Using a dry-erase marker on a mirror, write out: *God wants me to experience joy.*

In verse 4, David instructed his readers to "sing to the Lord." The next step in the sequence after forgiveness is worship. Write your own psalm of praise to God for His forgiveness. Don't worry about making it rhyme or giving it a certain number of lines, just express your praise in written form.

day 24

A THIN LINE

━━━━━━━━

discover |

Sometimes joy closely follows pain. Think about the pain of running a 5k and the joy of crossing the finish line. Or the pain of working all summer to save up for the prom dress you always dreamed about. Or maybe even the pain of fearing rejection and the joy of finding a new friend. There might be pain—emotional and physical—along the way, but the end of the journey is worth it. This connection of pain and joy gives us a better understanding of what Jesus experienced on the cross.

READ

HEBREWS 12:1-2.

For the joy that lay before him, he endured the cross, despising the shame, and sat down at the right hand of the throne of God. —Hebrews 12:2b

Jesus never experienced worse pain than the cross. He had the weight of all the world's sins upon Him and the pain of separation from His Father. Yet, He endured the cross because of the joy that came after it. Above all, He looked forward to the joy of pleasing His Father. The joy of making a way for us to be saved. The joy of being glorified for eternity in heaven (Rev. 4:8). For Jesus, the joy of doing His Father's will outweighed the pain, so He willingly laid down His own life. Just like Jesus did, we can endure the pain in life, knowing that eternal joy is on the other side.

Thank Jesus for being willing to endure the pain of the cross. Without His willingness to face that pain, we would not have an opportunity to be saved.

delight |

There will be points in your life where the path to joy leads through pain. When you find yourself here, remember Jesus.

Describe a time in your life when you had to walk through pain before you could experience joy. What was your biggest encouragement to keep on despite the pain?

Sometimes pain comes from persecution. Have you ever felt persecution for your faith in Jesus? How did the Holy Spirit help you?

Hebrews 12:1 mentioned the "large cloud of witnesses." These are our Christian brothers and sisters who have gone before us. How does it feel to know that they are cheering you on right now from heaven?

display |

Hebrews 12:2 mentioned Jesus being seated at the right hand of God. The place on the right hand side of a king was for a person of highest rank.[8] As believers, Jesus must have the highest ranking place in our lives.

How does your life show that Jesus is the most important person in your life?

What are some ways focusing on Jesus might help you through tough times?

No Matter What

Trust in the LORD with all your heart, and do not rely on your own understanding; in all your ways know him,

& HE WILL MAKE YOUR PATHS STRAIGHT.

PROVERBS 3:5-6

day 25

A HOPEFUL FUTURE

discover |

We can be joyful, even when it's difficult, but depression is also a real issue. Yes, even people who love Jesus can be depressed. Thankfully, we also have an eternal hope that is anchored much deeper than our feelings. Our hope is anchored in Jesus Christ, the Son of the one true God. And God has better plans for us than we can imagine, even when all we think we see ahead is pain.

READ

JEREMIAH 29:10-14.

"For I know the plans I have for you"—this is the LORD's declaration—"plans for your well-being, not for disaster, to give you a future and a hope."
—Jeremiah 29:11

While you might be familiar with this verse, its context is often overlooked. Jeremiah was writing to the Jews who had just been conquered and deported from their homeland. They were a broken people who had 70 more years of living in another country under the rule of a foreign king. But right in the middle of this scriptural "reality check" is a beautiful declaration of hope.

Essentially, God said, "I know what you're going through, and I have plans for you that are better than you can imagine." Believing this is step one of what we do when being joyful is difficult. We have to remember that God is good. We have to know— regardless of our circumstances—God has a plan for us and His plan is not to bring disaster on us, but to give us a hopeful future.

delight |

Finding joy in whatever circumstances we face deeply trusting in God and His goodness.

Ask yourself: *Do I believe God is good? Do I believe He has a plan for me? Do I believe His aim is for my ultimate good and not disaster?*

How do you reconcile the difficulties of life with the goodness of God?

display |

When it's difficult to feel joyful, Jeremiah says we should certainly trust in God's goodness, but we should also pray. This isn't a half-hearted, routine, or silent prayer; it's a crying out to God from the depths of your soul (Rom. 8:26). God promises that you *will* find Him "when you search for me with all your heart" (Jer. 29:13).

What does it look like to search for God with your whole heart, even when you're struggling to feel joyful?

Dwell on the goodness of God. Write out a prayer of confession. Confess where you've doubted God's goodness. Confess where you've struggled to find joy. Ultimately, confess that you love Him and trust Him. Then, write out one prayer request for someone you know is struggling to trust God's goodness and present it to Him in prayer.

No Matter What

day 26

SPOILER ALERT

discover |

Are you ever tempted to skip to the last few pages of a book to see how everything ends? Or do you read the episode descriptions for the show you're binging on Netflix, just to get a hint of where the story goes? Most of us have probably wanted to do this before—and maybe we did.

Jesus understood this desire and gave His disciples a glimpse of what their future would look like. He didn't tell them the full story, but shared enough for them to know the theme of their future.

READ
JOHN 16:31-33.

"I have told you these things so that in me you may have peace. You will have suffering in this world. Be courageous! I have conquered the world."
—John 16:33

Jesus was just hours away from being arrested, falsely accused, and crucified. He knew the end was near. As He was giving His disciples some final instructions and encouragement, He tried to spell it out very clearly for them, "Guys, I'm going away, but I'll be back." This didn't sink in for His disciples, though. So then Jesus dropped the ultimate spoiler: "be courageous! I have conquered the world" (v. 33).

Here's the thing: Jesus hadn't gone to the cross yet. He hadn't been resurrected yet. He hadn't ascended into heaven yet. But He knew what was coming. So He could say, "I have conquered the world" (v. 33).

That same Jesus who had the certainty to say He had conquered the world before His death, burial, resurrection, and ascension, is the same Jesus who is in charge of your life today. When you think about it from that angle, tackling the whole, "Be courageous!" part becomes a lot easier.

delight |

When Jesus said He conquered the world, it doesn't mean He took over or defeated the world with military force. Rather, it means He won the victory over sin and death (1 Cor. 15:55-57).

How does knowing Jesus conquered sin and death bring you joy?

Jesus also said that we will have suffering in this world (v. 33). How does knowing that He has conquered the world help you have joy even in seasons of suffering?

display |

Although we might want to keep the spoilers to ourselves when it comes to books, movies, and TV shows, we don't have to do that with God's story. In fact, we're called to share His story from beginning to end.

Who can you talk with about the joy you've found in Jesus? When you have this conversation, it's okay to be real. You don't have to sugar-coat anything. Instead, let them know that following Christ isn't easy, but it still brings joy.

Ask God to help you know who to share with about the joy of Jesus.

day 27

discover|

Sometimes even our faith heroes have moments of despair—including even John the Baptist. This is the guy Jesus described by saying, "among those born of women no one greater than John the Baptist has appeared" (Matt. 11:11). But a few verses earlier, as John sat in a prison cell, he had a moment of doubt. He asked his followers to talk to Jesus and make sure that He really was the Messiah. Jesus didn't get onto them. Instead, He scolded those who didn't believe John's message of preparation for the Messiah. (See Luke 7:18-23.)

READ

MATTHEW 11:28-30.

"Come to me, all of you who are weary and burdened, and I will give you rest.
Take up my yoke and learn from me, because I am lowly and humble in heart,
and you will find rest for your souls. For my yoke is easy and my burden is light."

When we don't feel like being joyful, we sometimes think God is made at us for having doubts. But the enemy uses and twists these thoughts to try to put distance between us and God. But we see the truth and Jesus hearts in His words to His followers all those years ago: "Come to me." He did not say, "come to me only if you have no doubts" or "come to me only those who have their if you have it all together," or even, "come to me only if you aren't struggling." He said come to me "all who are weary and burdened." That includes doubters, mess-ups, and strugglers. No matter where you are on your faith journey, the call to come extends to you.

---

delight |

Jesus wasn't saying following Him is easy. In fact, He went out of His way in other places to say how difficult it would be (Matt. 10:22). What He was trying to show is that He empathizes with our pain. He knows what it's like to be human, and He is there for us (Heb. 4:15).

You don't have to change anything about yourself before you come to Jesus. How does this truth comfort and encourage you?

How has the enemy tried to put distance between you and God?

display |

It's true that Jesus calls us just as we are, but He doesn't want us to stay just as we are. He wants us to grow to be more like Him. Think about your life over the last year. Write out three ways you're more like Christ. Then, write out three ways you need to submit yourself more fully to Him.

Thank God that Jesus understands our needs but still allows us to come to Him and find peace and joy.

No Matter What

day 28

TRUST GOD

---

discover |

Every story has a conflict to be resolved by the end. Somewhere along the way, our hero or heroine is advised: "Just follow your heart." Somehow, everything turns out okay. That sounds like most *Hallmark* movies, right? But it doesn't align with God's Word.

READ

PROVERBS 3:1-11.

Trust in the LORD with all your heart, and do not rely on your own understanding; in all your ways know him, and he will make your paths straight.
—Proverbs 3:5-6

Scripture actually warns us to do the opposite: Do not trust your heart—it's flawed and deceitful (Jer. 17:9). Our hearts often tell us to look out for ourselves, to pursue our dreams and desires no matter the cost. Our hearts tell us to run and hide when we're scared. Our hearts even whisper lies to us. When we're struggling to find joy, listening to our hearts is usually the last thing we should do.

Instead, Scripture tells us to trust in the Lord wholeheartedly rather than trusting our own understanding. When we know God, we trust Him to guide us on the right path and follow His lead. This is the opposite of what the world tells us, but it leads out of despair and into joy.

Think about your life. Where you've followed God's path, thank Him for His direction. Where have you chosen to try your own way? Ask for forgiveness in those areas.

---

delight |

When has following your heart led you down a painful path?

How did God bring you back to a place of joy? If you aren't there yet, ask Him to restore your joy.

What are some ways you can grow in your relationship with God, trusting Him and following Him on whatever path He sets before you?

display |

There are many ways to grow in your relationship with God, and one of the best ways is Scripture memory.

Re-write Proverbs 3:5-6 in your own words.

Use pages 62-63 to guide you as you try to memorize these verses.

Learning to completely lean on God rather than our understand takes practice. One way to practice this is by praying before we make important decisions. Whenever you face an important decision this week, pray first. If God leads you to choose something other than what you wanted, ask Him to help you find joy anyway and to believe that He has your best interest in mind.

day 29

---

discover |

One of the greatest comforts we have when other believers die is knowing that we will see them again. We know that their life isn't over; in fact it's just beginning. Christians are comforted by the knowledge that they are with Jesus.

READ
JOHN 16:19-22.

"So you also have sorrow now. But I will see you again. Your hearts will rejoice, and no one will take away your joy from you." —John 16:22

Jesus knew He was about to be leaving the disciples, first through His death, then again after His resurrection through His ascension back into heaven. He knew that His crucifixion would seem like the end of the world for His followers, but would seem like a great victory for those who opposed Him. He knew He would return from the grave, and no one could take away the joy His disciples would feel.

This reality is the same for us two thousand years later. Jesus has risen, and He is coming again. On that day, we will finally see Him. When we struggle to find joy, this is what sustains us. We have to know that this is not the final stop on our journey.

Of course we want to enjoy our time on Earth, but on the rough days, we have to trust that better days are ahead. We can hold onto this hope because we know Jesus will return one day—and on that day, all sorrow, pain, and suffering will stop (Rev. 21:3-8).

delight |

Unlike the disciples, we've never seen Jesus with our own eyes, but we believe in Him.

What sustains your belief in Jesus?

How does knowing that He will return help you remain joyful, even when it's tough?

Talk honestly with the Lord about where you are today. Are you filled with despair or joy? Ask Him to remind you that He will return and one day make all things new.

display |

The hardest part of waiting is not knowing when Jesus will return and make all things new.

Write out two ways you will strive to live in joy, knowing Jesus will return and we will see Him.

The joy we'll have when Jesus returns will be everlasting. Write out one sentence expressing how much you are looking forward to that day. Find someone to share this joy with today.

day 30

ALWAYS

discover|

We will all have bad days, disappointments, and maybe even seasons of depression. But God has given us tools to help us find joy no matter what we're facing. Most of all, Jesus' promises to us can sustain us even on the darkest of days.

READ

MATTHEW 28.

"And remember, I am with you always, to the end of the age."
—Matthew 28:20b

There are two promises in this chapter that encourage us to remain joyful no matter what's going on in our lives.

Jesus is alive. The angel at Jesus' empty tomb told the ladies not to be afraid (v. 5). But it's not enough just to try to not be afraid, we need to know why we shouldn't fear: Jesus has risen from the grave (v. 6). We don't have to be afraid anymore because Jesus is alive.

Jesus is with us. No matter what we go through, how challenging things may be, how dark life seems: Jesus is always with us. Because Jesus is alive and with us, we can walk with confidence through our days.

Real, sustaining joy comes entirely from these two truths. Because these two things are true, we have life, hope, and joy— inexpressible and unattainable for those who do not know Christ. And we're called to share the reason for this hope and joy with everyone we meet (1 Pet. 3:15).

Spend a few minutes thanking God for Jesus. Thank Him for the resurrection, and thank Jesus for His continued presence in your life.

delight |

How might focusing on Jesus' resurrection keep you from being afraid?

How does knowing that Jesus is alive and with you give you confidence to face whatever comes your way?

display |

Spending time in the Bible or reading a devotion on joy doesn't mean you'll always be super joyful. But it will show you the way God's Word defines true joy, along with how to seek it, sustain it, and share it with others.

List three key takeaways from studying joy.

What's one thing about joy can you share with someone else that might increase their joy?

JOY IN THESE PAGES
How faith heroes handled despair.

Traditionally in the church, Christians have often felt like it was wrong for them to feel down or struggle with seasons of depression. Today, we understand that depression is the result of a fallen world—and while it may result from personal sin, this isn't always the case. As with all of life's biggest questions, we turn to our ultimate source of truth—God's Word—for the answer.

The Bible doesn't diagnose any of our faith heroes with depression as a consistent mental health issue. But we do know that countless biblical characters experienced moments or seasons of darkness and despair—including Jesus Himself. By studying their lives on the pages of Scripture, we can learn how to fight depression from a spiritual perspective. We can experience true and lasting joy.

ELIJAH
Read 1 Kings 19.

After God's powerful display with the prophets of Baal, Jezebel threatened Elijah, and He ran in fear. Once he reached the wilderness, he cried out to God: "I have had enough! Lord, take my life" (1 Kings 19:4). Elijah felt alone and afraid; He was so distraught that he wished for death. God responded by first taking care of Elijah's needs for food and rest, then God gave Elijah the gift of His presence on the mountain (vv. 11-12). Only then did God send Elijah forward to anoint Elisha to be his help and successor.

DAVID
Read Psalm 13:1-6; 55:4-5; 69:1-36.

If you look at the Davidic Psalms, it won't take long to see that David experienced countless victories and days of despair. He went from hiding from a king bent on killing him, to becoming king himself, to having an affair and committing murder, to repentance and restoration. With David, it's important to note that moments of his despair were related to his own sin, so his response to that was rightly his repentance (Ps. 51:1-19). But when the circumstances were beyond His control, he still cried out to God: "How long, Lord? Will you forget me forever? … How long will I store up anxious concerns within me, agony in my mind every day?" (Ps. 13:1-2). Interestingly, even when David began a Psalm with despair, he typically ended in praise, affirming his trust in God (Ps. 13:5-6).

JOB
Read Job 1-3, focusing on 3:1-7,11-12; 42:1-17.

Job's life was turned upside down—he lost everything he owned, along with livestock, servants, and even children. The Bible calls his suffering "very intense" (Job 2:13). His friends assumed it was the result of sin, and his wife told him to curse God and die. But Job said no. While Job remained faithful to God in every trial, he also "cursed the day he was born" (Job 3:1). God allowed Job to suffer before He stepped in, but God didn't leave Job alone in this time of tragedy. God reminded Job of who He was. Job's response is one we should strive to imitate in times of despair: "I know that you can do anything and no plan of yours can be thwarted. … I reject my words and am sorry for them" (Job 42:2,6). He humbly recognized what God spoke through the prophet Isaiah: "my ways are higher than your ways, and my thoughts than your thoughts" (Isa. 55:9). Then God restored Job's possessions, gave him more children, and blessed Him immensely (Job 42:10,12).

JEREMIAH
Read Jeremiah 15:10-11 and Lamentations 3:14-20,22-26.

Aside from the fact that Jeremiah wrote an entire book titled Lamentations (a lament is a passionate expression of grief or sorrow), he actually said he had "become depressed" (Lam. 3:20). Jeremiah was alone and rejected, and people even planned to harm him. He cried out to God many times throughout his ministry, even angrily asking why his pain was "unending" (Jer. 15:18). God responded to Jeremiah, asking him to repent of his anger, while also assuring Jeremiah that he would be safe (Jer. 15:19-21). Jeremiah responded by asking God for healing (Jer. 17:14). Much like David, Jeremiah often expressed his troubled heart to the Lord, then returned to praise (Lam. 3:20-26).

JESUS
Read Isaiah 53:3-5; Hebrews 4:15; and Luke 22:40-46.

Before you declare this statement heretical, this is not a claim that Jesus was depressed—far from it. Rather, this is a claim that Jesus experienced deep sadness, just like we do (Isa. 53:3; Heb. 4:12). Just before He was arrested, He cried out to His Father, asking if there was another way. He prayed so fervently that "his sweat became like drops of blood"(Luke 22:44). As He became sin on the cross, He cried out to His Father in despair, "My God, my God, why have you abandoned me" (Matt. 27:46). The way Jesus responded to His suffering teaches us about our greatest weapons for fighting darkness.

WHAT WE CAN LEARN

Though these are only short summaries of the lives of these Bible heroes, we can learn the key to driving the darkness of depression right out of our lives. Every single one of these people cried out to God for help—or in repentance if necessary—then they continued walking the path God had called them to. Let's take a look at some specific ways we can imitate their example when we face seasons of despair.

Acknowledge God. Like Job, recognize that as God, the Father has the right to give or take whatever He wants (1:21); that He can do anything and His plans will always move forward (Job 42:2). We can also submit to His authority and say, "not my will, but yours, be done" like Jesus did (Luke 22:42).

Pray. When life gets you down cry out to God. Tell Him exactly how you're struggling. Elijah told God that he wanted to die. David asked God to answer him and be compassionate (Ps. 69:16). Job said he'd asked for help and God didn't answer (30:20). Jeremiah expressed his anger, saying he felt like God was "a mirage" (15:18). And Jesus asked, "if you are willing, take this cup away from me" (Luke 22:42). While we should always approach God with the reverence He deserves, we can open our hearts to Him. He's the only One who can truly bring light and healing.

Praise. It's common practice to praise God when He brings us out of a season of despair, but what people like David show is how to praise (delight in) Him even when we feel down. Though David occasionally asked things like where God was or for God to save him from his enemies, he circled back to praise God for who He is. And if we look at Jeremiah, just two verses after saying he was depressed, he affirmed that God's "mercies never end" (Lam. 3:22).

Surround yourself with people who care. We know that the first step is taking our cares to God, but it also helps to talk with compassionate others. You need to find people who will carry your burdens with you. God provided Elisha to help Elijah, and to eventually take over Elijah's ministry. Job's friends—although they gave bad advice—did give him their presence. Jesus shared His heart with His disciples, asking them to pray for Him. We can see the negative effects of not having these people in the fact that Jeremiah had no family or friends, and he is often called "the weeping prophet."

Keep doing the work God has called you to do. Elijah continued to prophesy. David continued to seek God and lead His people. Job continued to believe God and serve Him in faithfulness. Jeremiah continued to call God's people to repentance and trusted God to take care of him. Jesus went to the cross, becoming our sin, dying to pay the price for it, and was resurrected.

REFLECT

What's the greatest truth you've seen from studying the lives of these characters of faith? How will you allow it to influence the way you respond to feeling down in the future?

If you're experiencing a season of darkness, take a minute to sit in God's presence and talk to Him. If you don't know where to start, remember that the Holy Spirit has words to pray for us when we have nothing left to give (Rom. 8:26-27). You can also use the prompt below to help you get started.

God, I recognize that You are God, that You are good and work all things for good for those who love You. I realize that when I respond in godly ways to my suffering, all of the praise and glory goes to You. Thank You for the ways You love, provide for, teach, and hear me. Help me to see You in every aspect of my day. Show me how to take my eyes off of my circumstances and shift my focus to where it belongs—on You. Help me to fully delight in You.

sources

1. Michael Jordan, Forbes Quotes: Thoughts on The Business of Life (Forbes), accessed September 4, 2020, https://www.forbes.com/quotes/11194/.
2. Edwin A. Blum and Trevin Wax, *CSB Study Bible* (Nashville, TN: Holman Bible Publishers, 2017), accessed via mywsb.com.
3. A.W. Geiger and Leslie Davis, "A Growing Number of American Teenagers – Particularly Girls – Are Facing Depression," Pew Research Center (Pew Research Center, May 30, 2020), https://www.pewresearch.org/fact-tank/2019/07/12/a-growing-number-of-american-teenagers-particularly-girls-are-facing-depression/.
4. "G4727 - Stenazō - Strong's Greek Lexicon (KJV)," Blue Letter Bible, accessed September 4, 2020, https://www.blueletterbible.org/lang/lexicon/lexicon.cfm?Strongs=G4727.
5. Adapted from Ronald Kessler, "Kessler Psychological Distress Scale (K10)," accessed September 18, 2020, http://www.aci.health.nsw.gov.au/__data/assets/pdf_file/0015/212901/Kessler_10_and_scoring.pdf; Ivan Goldberg, "Depression Test - Do You Have Depression?" Psychology Tests & Quizzes, accessed August 31, 2020, https://psychcentral.com/quizzes/depression-quiz/.
6. "Delight," Merriam-Webster (Merriam-Webster), accessed September 4, 2020, https://www.merriam-webster.com/dictionary/delight.
7. Alexander Pope, *An Essay on Man* (United Kingdom: A. Millar, and J. and R. Tonson, 1767), 10.
8. "What Is the Significance of the Right Hand of God?," accessed September 9, 2020, https://www.compellingtruth.org/right-hand-of-God.html.